A
CHRISTMAS
Treasury

A COLLECTION OF
CAROLS, RECIPES,
GAMES & MEMORIES

Elm Hill Books®
An Imprint of J. Countryman®

A Christmas Treasury
ISBN: 1-4041-8510-0

The quoted ideas expressed in this book (but not scripture verses) are not, in all cases, exact quotations, as some have been edited for clarity and brevity. In all cases, the author has attempted to maintain the speaker's original intent. In some cases, quoted material for this book was obtained from secondary sources, primarily print media. While every effort was made to ensure the accuracy of these sources, the accuracy cannot be guaranteed.

Scripture quotations marked NKJV are taken from *The Holy Bible, New King James Version*. Copyright © 1982 by Thomas Nelson, Inc. Used by permission.

Manuscript written and compiled by Rebecca Currington in association with Snapdragon Editorial Group, Inc.

Cover and interior pages designed by D/SR Design, LLC.

*C*hristmas is more than a day or a season; it's the foundation stone of our hope in God's love for us. It's the celebration of God's greatest gift—a Savior—sent in the form of a tiny babe in a hay-filled crèche. Christmas is first, last, and always about Jesus.

In the pages of this little book, we have included the essence of Christmas—the story of Christ's lowly birth and the remarkable heavenly celebration that accompanied it. We've also provided a sampling of the simple joys we share in remembrance of that glorious event—carols, games, stories, recipes, verse, and inspirational quotes. We hope *A Christmas Treasury* will touch your heart and cause you to give thanks for the holy child who brought us "Peace on earth, goodwill toward men!"

THE CHRISTMAS STORY
Luke 2:1-20 NKJV

*A*nd it came to pass in those days that a decree went out from Caesar Augustus that all the world should be registered. This census first took place while Quirinius was governing Syria. So all went to be registered, everyone to his own city.

Joseph also went up from Galilee, out of the city of Nazareth, into Judea, to the city of David, which is called Bethlehem, because he was of the house and lineage of David, to be registered with Mary, his betrothed wife, who was with child. So it was, that while they were there, the days were completed for her to be delivered. And she brought forth her firstborn Son, and wrapped Him in swaddling cloths, and laid Him in a manger, because there was no room for them in the inn.

Now there were in the same country shepherds living out in the fields, keeping watch over their flock by night. And behold, an angel of the Lord stood before them, and the glory of the Lord shone around them, and they were greatly afraid. Then the angel said to them, "Do not be afraid, for behold, I bring you good tidings of great joy which will be to all people. For there is born to you this day in the city of David a Savior, who is Christ the Lord. And this will be the sign to you: You will find a Babe wrapped in swaddling cloths, lying in a manger."

So it was, when the angels had gone away from them into heaven, that the shepherds said to one another, "Let us now go to Bethlehem and see this thing that has come to pass, which the Lord has made known to us." And they came with haste and found Mary and Joseph, and the Babe lying in a manger.

Now when they had seen Him, they made widely known the saying which was told them concerning this Child. And all those who heard it marveled at those things which were told them by the shepherds. But Mary kept all these things and pondered them in her heart. Then the shepherds returned, glorifying and praising God for all the things that they had heard and seen.

Thanks be to God for His indescribable gift!

2 CORINTHIANS 9:15 NKJV

The shepherds sing; and shall I silent be?
My God, no hymn for Thee?
My soul's a shepherd too: a flock it feeds
Of thoughts, and words, and deeds.
The pasture is Thy Word, the streams, Thy Grace
Enriching all the place,
Shepherd and flock shall sing, and all my powers
Out-sing the daylight hours.

GEORGE HERBERT

Shepherds at the grange,
Where the Babe was born,
Sang with many a change,
Christmas carols until morn.

HENRY WADSWORTH LONGFELLOW

CHRISTMAS FUN—SANTA HAT SNATCH

Hand out a Santa hat to each person.

Announce the following:

No one can remove his or her hat until you have removed yours.

Don't be the last person left wearing your hat.

Let another game or conversation take place, and as time goes by, people will take their attention off you and forget the game is happening. Eventually, remove your hat and watch as people catch on and snatch theirs off their heads. Eventually, one unsuspecting person will be left. This person is the big "Loser!" When the loser is acknowledged, put the hats back on and begin the game again, this time with the loser as leader.

MERRY BERRY CHRISTMAS PUNCH

¹/₂ gallon orange juice
1 large bottle cranberry or cranberry/apple juice
2 cups white grapefruit juice
1 cup blackberry syrup
1 sliced orange
1 sliced lime

Combine ingredients and chill. After pouring into the punchbowl, add the lemon and lime slices to the top.

IRISH CAROL
(Christmas Day Has Come)

Christmas Day has come; let's prepare for mirth,
Which fills the heavens and earth at the amazing birth.
Through both the joyous angels in strife and hurry fly,
With glory and hosannas 'All Holy' do they cry,
In heaven the Church triumphant adores with all her choirs,
The militant on earth with humble faith admires.

But why should we rejoice? Should we not rather morn
To see the Hope of Nations thus in a stable born?
Where are His crown and scepter, where is His throne sublime,
Where is his train majestic that should the stars outshine?
Is there no sumptuous palace, nor any inn at all
To lodge his heavenly mother but in a filthy stall?

*O*h! Cease, ye blessed angels, such clamorous joys to make!
Though midnight silence favors, the shepherds are awake;
And you, O glorious star! That with new splendor brings,
From the remotest parts three learned eastern kings,
Turn somewhere else your luster, your rays elsewhere display,
For Herod he may slay the babe, and Christ must straight away.

If we would then rejoice, let's cancel the old score,
And purposing amendment, resolve to sin no more—
For mirth can ne'er content us, without a conscience clear;
And thus we'll find true pleasure in all the usual cheer,
In dancing, sporting, reveling, with masquerade and drum,
So let our Christmas merry be, as Christmas doth become.[1]

Also known as "Christmas Day Is Come," "Irish Carol" is most commonly attributed to Bishop Luke Wadding (1588–1657) of Wexford, Ireland. This folk carol has also been attributed to Fr. William Devereaux from around 1728.[2]

En Clara Vox
(A Thrilling Voice by Jordan Rings)

A thrilling voice by Jordan rings,
rebuking guilt and darksome things:
vain dreams of sin and visions fly;
Christ in His might shines forth on high.

Now let each torpid soul arise,
that sunk in guilt and wounded lies;
see! The new Star's refulgent ray
shall chase disease and sin away.

The Lamb descends from heaven above
to pardon sin with freest love:
for such indulgent mercy shewn
with tearful joy our thanks we own.

*T*hat when again He shines revealed,
and trembling worlds to terror yield.
He give not sin its just reward,
but in His love protect and guard.

To the most high Parent glory be
and to the Son be victory,
and to the Spirit praise is owed
from age to age eternally. Amen.[3]

Written in the sixth century, *Vox Clara* literally means, "hymn for Lauds in Advent," Lauds meaning "praises." This traditional song of praise recalls the proclamation by John the Baptist, that he was "the voice of one crying in the wilderness" as he cried out, "Prepare ye the way of the Lord." (Matthew 3:1, 3 KJV.)[4]

Adeste Fidelis
(O Come All Ye Faithful)

O come all ye faithful, joyful and triumphant,
O come ye, o come ye, to Bethlehem!
Come and behold Him, born the King of angels!

O come, let us adore Him,
O come, let us adore Him,
O come, let us adore Him,
Christ the Lord!

Sing, choirs of angels, sing in exultation,
O sing, all ye citizens of heaven above!
Glory to God, glory in the highest!

O come, let us adore Him,
O come, let us adore Him,
O come, let us adore Him,
Christ the Lord!

Yea, Lord, we greet Thee, born this happy morning,
Jesus to Thee be all glory giv'n;
Word of the Father, now in flesh appearing!

O come, let us adore Him,
O come, let us adore Him,
O come, let us adore Him,
Christ the Lord![5]

Considered by some to be an anonymous Latin hymn, others attribute this beautiful carol to John F. Wade, a Catholic layman who fled the Jacobean rebellion in 1745, settling in Douay, France. It is thought that Wade put the text to music, which was probably composed by Englishman John Reading around 1751. In 1853, today's popular translation first appeared and is attributed to Rev. Frederick Oakley.[6]

O TANNENBAUM
(O Christmas Tree)

O Christmas tree, O Christmas tree!
How are thy leaves so verdant!
O Christmas tree, O Christmas tree,
How are thy leaves so verdant!
Not only in the summertime,
But even in winter is thy prime.
O Christmas tree, O Christmas tree,
How are thy leaves so verdant!

O Christmas tree, O Christmas tree,
Much pleasure doth thou bring me!
O Christmas tree, O Christmas tree,
Much pleasure doth thou bring me!
For every year the Christmas tree,
Brings to us all both joy and glee.
O Christmas tree, O Christmas tree,
Much pleasure doth thou bring me!

O Christmas tree, O Christmas tree,
Thy candles shine out brightly!
O Christmas tree, O Christmas tree,
Thy candles shine out brightly!
Each bough doth hold its tiny light,
That makes each toy to sparkle bright.
O Christmas tree, O Christmas tree,
Thy candles shine out brightly![7]

This carol, also called "O Christmas Tree," is of German origin, penned in 1824 by a Leipzig organist named Ernst Anschütz. A Tannenbaum is a fir tree *(die Tanne)*, a popular choice for Christmas trees *(der Weihnachtsbaum)* in Germany and throughout the world. Although other kinds of evergreens are used as well, it is, nonetheless, the Tannenbaum that has inspired many German songs, the lyrics of the first dating back to 1550. Quite interestingly, the familiar melody that we use for the carol today is also used by Iowa, Maryland, Michigan, and New Jersey for their state songs, Maryland's opening line being "Maryland, O Maryland."[8]

THE FIRST NOEL

*T*he first Noel the angel did say
Was to certain poor shepherds in fields as they lay;
In fields as they lay, keeping their sheep,
On a cold winter's night that was so deep.

Noel, Noel, Noel, Noel,
Born is the King of Israel.

They looked up and saw a star
Shining in the east beyond them far,
And to the earth it gave great light,
And so it continued both day and night.

And by the light of that same star
Three wise men came from country far;
To seek for a king was their intent,
And to follow the star wherever it went.

*T*his star drew nigh to the northwest,
O'er Bethlehem it took its rest,
And there it did both stop and stay
Right over the place where Jesus lay.

Then entered in those wise men three
Fall reverently upon their knee,
And offered there in His presence
Their gold, and myrrh, and frankincense.

Then let us all with one accord
Sing praises to our heavenly Lord;
That hath made heaven and earth of naught,
And with his blood mankind hath bought.[9]

This carol most likely dates back to the 16th or 17th century but could possibly be from the 13th. It is thought to be of French origin by some; whereas others hold that it is English, originally spelled *Nowell*. It has also been described as "A Carol for the Epiphany" and first appeared in *Christmas Carols Ancient and Modern*, a collection of William Sandys', dated 1833.[10]

Christmas Goodies—Stuffed Dates

1 (3 oz.) package cream cheese, softened
2 Tbsp. powdered sugar
1-2 Tbsp. orange juice
$\frac{1}{4}$ cup chopped walnuts
1 (6 oz.) package pitted dates

Beat cream cheese until creamy. Add powered sugar and enough orange juice to make a creamy stuffing consistency. Stir in walnuts. Make a lengthwise slit in dates. Stuff dates with cream cheese mixture.

Yield: 4 dozen

THE LITTLE LOAF
Adapted from McGuffey's Third Reader

A long and devastating famine meant a meager Christmas for the children in the town. As an act of kindness, a rich baker sent for twenty of the poorest chidlren in the town and said to them, "In this basket there is a loaf for each of you. Take it, and come back to me every day until God sends us better times."

The hungry children gathered eagerly about the basket and quarreled over the bread—each eager to have the largest loaf. At last they went away without even thanking the good man.

But Gretchen, a poorly dressed little girl, did not quarrel or struggle with the rest. Instead, she stood modestly waiting about a pace away. When the ill-behaved children left, she took the smallest loaf, which alone was left in the basket, kissed the man's hand, and went home.

The next day the children were as ill-behaved as before, and poor, timid Gretchen received a loaf scarecely half the size of the one she had received the day before. When she came home, and her mother cut the loaf open, however, something amazing happened. Many new, shining pieces of silver fell out onto the table.

*G*retchen's mother was greatly alarmed. "Take the money back to the good baker at once," she told Gretchen. "These coins must have fallen into the dough by accident. Go Gretchen. Go quickly," she urged, greatly afraid that they would be accused of thievery. But when the little girl returned to the baker with the coins and told him what her mother had said, he assured her that the coins had not fallen into the dough by accident. He had carefully placed them there himself.

"I had the silver pieces put into the smallest loaf to reward you," said the baker. "Go home now and help your mother prepare a fine Christmas dinner. Tell your mother that the money is your own to keep." And then, patting her on the head, he said, "Gretchen, dear, you are a precious child. I hope that you will always be as contented, peaceable, and grateful as you are now."

The End

*T*he joy of brightening each others' lives, bearing each others' burdens, easing each others' loads, and supplanting empty hearts and lives with generous gifts becomes for us the magic of Christmas.

W. C. JONES

Products from Elm Hill Books may be purchased in bulk for educational, business, fundraising, or sales promotional use. For information, please email SpecialMarkets@ThomasNelson.com.

For additions, deletions, corrections, or clarifications in future editions of this text, please email ContactUs@ElmHillBooks.com.

1   Lyrics found at http://www.lutheran-hymnal.com/german/irish_carol.htm (accessed February 2005).

2   Ibid.

3   Lyrics found at http://home.earthlink.net/~thesaurus/thesaurus/Hymni/VoxClara.html (accessed February 2005).

4   Ibid.; http://www.anonymous4.com/yool.htm; and http://www.newadvent.org/cathen/03724b.htm (accessed February 2005).

5   The *Baptist Hymnal* (Nashville, TN: Convention Press, 1956) no. 66.

6   Ibid.; http://www.cyberhymnal.org/bio/w/a/d/wade_jf.htm (accessed February 2005); and http://www3.pair.com/montrsmu/carolshist/ocome.html (accessed February 2005).

7   Lyrics found at http://www.santas.net/ochristmastree.htm (accessed February 2005).

8   Information found at http://www.serve.com/shea/germusa/xmastree.htm and http://german.about.com/library/blotannenb.htm (accessed February 2005).

9   Lyrics found at http://www.41051.com/xmaslyrics/firstnoel.html (accessed February 2005).

10 Information found in the *Baptist Hymnal*, no. 63; http://www3.pair.com/montrsmu/caroshist/noel.html; and http://www.hymnsandcarolsofchristmas.com/Hymns_and_Carols/first_nowell.htm (accessed February 2005).